A
Pocket
Guide to

Lāna'i

An Island Apart

Library of Congress Catalog Card Number: 2003100295

ISBN-10: 1-56647-593-7
ISBN-13: 978-1-56647-593-8

First Printing, July 2003
Second Printing, May 2006
2 3 4 5 6 7 8 9

Design by Mardee Domingo Melton

Except where otherwise credited, all photos in this book are by Joe West.

Mutual Publishing, LLC
1215 Center Street, Suite 210
Honolulu, Hawai'i 96816
Ph: (808) 732-1709 Fax: (808) 734-4094
e-mail: mutual@mutualpublishing.com
www.mutualpublishing.com
Printed in Taiwan

A

Pocket

Guide to

Lāna'i

An Island Apart

WRITTEN BY
**Marcia Zina Mager
and Dennis Aubrey**

MAJOR PHOTOGRAPHY BY
Joe West

Mutual Publishing

Lāna'i at a Glance

COUNTY Maui

COUNTY SEAT Wailuku, Maui

LAND AREA 141 square miles, 89,000 acres

RESIDENT POPULATION 3,000

HIGHEST POINT Lāna'ihale, 3,370 feet

SHORELINE 47 miles

EXTREME LENGTH & WIDTH 18 miles long, 13 miles wide

AVERAGE ANNUAL TEMPERATURE (Lāna'i City) 71-77 degrees F

AVERAGE ANNUAL RAINFALL 4-5 inches coastline; over 20 inches city; 45 inches higher slopes

CHIEF INDUSTRIES Tourism and agriculture

PUBLIC & PRIVATE GOLF COURSES 3

PUBLIC TENNIS COURTS 1

PARKS 2 (Dole Park and Hulopo'e Beach)

HOTELS 3 (363 rooms)

MOST POPULAR VISITOR ATTRACTIONS

Hulopo'e Beach Park

Lāna'ihale

Kaiolohia (Shipwreck Beach)

Keahikawelo (Garden of the Gods)

Kānepu'u Preserve

KAIOHLOHIA
(Shipwreck Beach)

HALE 'O LONO

KAENA POINT

KEAHIKAWELO
(Garden of the Gods)

HONOPU BAY

Kaumalapau Harbor

Pali Kaholo

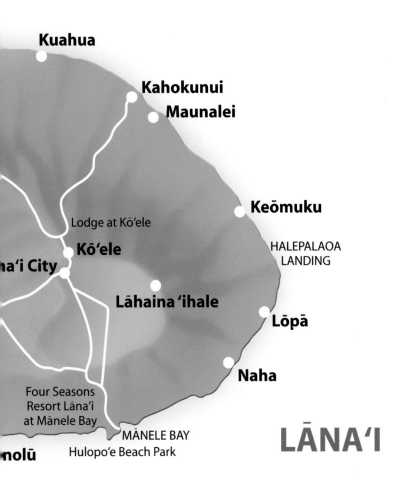

Kuahua

Kahokunui

Maunalei

Keōmuku

Lodge at Kōʻele

HALEPALAOA
LANDING

Kōʻele

na'i City

Lāhaina ʻihale

Lōpā

Naha

Four Seasons
Resort Lāna'i
at Mānele Bay

MĀNELE BAY
Hulopoʻe Beach Park

LĀNAʻI

nolū

Useful Local Phone Numbers

LĀNA'I AIRPORT
808-565-6757

LĀNA'I COMMUNITY HOSPITAL 24-HOUR EMERGENCY SERVICE
808-565-6411

LĀNA'I FAMILY HEALTH CENTER
808-565-6423

FIRST HAWAIIAN BANK
808-565-6969

BANK OF HAWAII
888-643-3888

POST OFFICE (Jacaranda Street)
808-565-6517

In addition, there's a Laundromat right off Dole Park in Lāna'i City, open 5:00 a.m. to 8:30 p.m. And a public library (808-565-7920) at 6th and Fraser, open Monday through Friday.

1,000-foot sea cliffs dominate the island's west coast.

Chapter One:
First Impressions

The plane dips below the thick clouds and an island shimmers below. To the left arcs one of the most spectacular coastline panoramas in Hawai'i, and to the right tower some of the tallest sea cliffs in the entire Pacific. And everywhere, stretching endlessly, are forgotten fields marked with lines of red earth, once home to thousands of acres of the world's best pineapple. As the descent begins towards the small modern airport, misty, verdant upper-mountain slopes loom into view.

Welcome to Lāna'i

For more than half a century, Lāna'i was known as "the pineapple island," serving as the world's largest source of pineapple, a plantation encompassing nearly 20,000 acres. But by the early 1990s, progress and passion transformed this third smallest Hawaiian island into a one-of-a-kind world-class resort destination. Lāna'i's new nickname, "the enticing island," fits like a glove. Nestled in a remote corner of Hawai'i, Lāna'i is 98 percent privately owned by Castle & Cooke and is finally being discovered by travelers from around the world. The island offers everything from authentically deserted white-sand beaches, untracked cloud forests, and sacred historical sites, to a pair of championship golf courses and two internationally acclaimed hotels. As if that weren't enough, Lāna'i is also home to 3,000 of the friendliest residents in the state.

> *Aia ka 'ike ia Polihua*
> *a lei i ka mānewanewa.*
>
> One proves a visit to Polihua by wearing a lei of mānewanewa.
>
> (A person proves his visit to a place by bringing back something native to the area. Refers to Polihua, Lāna'i.)

The last rays of another glorious Hawai'i day break through the clouds over the island of Lāna'i.

From outdoor wooden jail cells to a country hardware store and friendly post office, Lānaʻi City is the epitome of small-town Hawaiʻi.

A few miles outside the airport waits sleepy Lānaʻi City, the only community on the island, dotted with candy-colored tin-roofed plantation homes and giant pine trees. Lānaʻi is much more a small town than a city. Plantation workers flocked here back in the 1920s from the Philippines, China, and Japan to work in the thriving pineapple business. Succeeding generations of those same laborers still live in Lānaʻi City. But, instead of toiling long hours in the hot fields, they now work in the tourism industry as employees of Four Seasons Resort Lānaʻi, staffing every department of the two major hotels.

Arriving in Lānaʻi City is a step back in time. Everything looks very much the same as it did in the plantation days. There are still no stoplights, nor neon signs, nor fast-food franchises, and not a single traffic jam. Drivers cruise slowly along the

The last remnant of old Keōmuku, a turn-of-the-century sugar plantation town.

Mondays on Lāna'i are pretty much like Sundays. Fathers take their children spearfishing. Or golfing. Residents go paddling or surfing. In the afternoon you see locals "talking story" at the post office. People leave their car keys dangling in the ignition and sometimes postal workers will tell you about your package when they bump into you at the supermarket.

Sure, there are two incredible resorts frequented by Hollywood celebrities, famous politicians, and royal families. Sure, there are critically acclaimed chefs, luxurious spas, and the unforgettable amenities you'd find anywhere in the world.

But there's something here you rarely find anywhere else: a palatable sense of peacefulness—a visceral, hold-it-in-the-palm-of-your-hand tranquility.

empty streets in dusty Jeeps and cars, waving to friends and strangers alike. There are, thankfully, ATM machines at the two banks, a renovated theater that shows first-run movies, quaint churches, several delightful family-run eating and shopping places, and a tiny police station that boasts a single wooden outdoor jail cell. There is also a small hospital and medical clinic. (But you can't actually give birth at the hospital, so very pregnant Lāna'ians must go to another island during their last stages of pregnancy.) On most nights, by 7 p.m., absolutely everything closes down.

It doesn't matter whether you're having dinner at one of the two formal dining rooms, or snorkeling with friends at Hulopo'e Beach's Marine Preserve, or hiking along the summit of Lāna'ihale. Everywhere and anywhere you go on Lāna'i it's there—an easiness, *(Continued on page 10.)*

From tin-roof plantation houses built in the 1920s to modern multimillion-dollar private residences, Lānaʻi is home to a fascinating and diverse group of people.

People love to do things the old-fashioned way on Lāna'i, whether walking around town or playing in the surf at the beach.

A bird's-eye view of the north side of Lāna'i City nestled 1,700 feet above sea level.

a contentment, an almost startling quality of calm.

In the end, visiting Lānaʻi is not really about the beautiful beaches, exotic forests, or spectacular coastline. It's not really about the brilliant reef or the fantastic fishing or championship golf courses. In the end it's about the feeling you get. The feeling you get when you look into the smiling faces of the people who live there. The feeling you get when you walk into the uncrowded stores and cafés. The feeling you get when you sit on the island's most popular beach, watching the sunset, and you almost have the whole place to yourself. This is what you carry home with you, that you reach for long after you're back at the office, back in the midst of your all-too-busy modern life.

One thing's for certain. You won't easily forget Lānaʻi. You won't forget her people or her beauty. You'll have tasted her *mana*, her spirit. And chances are you'll be back for more.

*Note: All prices in this section and throughout the book are subject to change.

How to Get There*

(And how to get around once you've arrived!)

AIRPLANE

If you personally know Bill Gates, who was married on Lānaʻi, you can always hop a ride on his private jet. Otherwise, your choices are limited to **Island Air** (Oahu 1-808-484-2222, Neighbor Islands 1-800-652-6541, North America, 1-800-323-3345, From all other locations, 1-808-484-2222, www.islandair.com). Island Air uses twin-engine propeller planes. These smaller planes bounce around a bit in stiff trade winds. But the flight takes about 25 minutes, depending on weather conditions. All flights to Lānaʻi connect via Honolulu, Oʻahu.

An Island Air flight arrives at Lāna'i's tiny, unhurried airport.

BOAT

Expeditions Lahaina/Lāna'i Passenger Ferry (1-800-695-2624, 1-808-661-3756, www.go-lanai.com) operates a United States Coast Guard-certified passenger vessel 365 days a year, five times a day, between Lahaina, Maui, and Mānele Bay harbor; kama'āina and children rates available. It takes about 45 minutes to make the 15-mile crossing. With outdoor seating, this is a terrific way to spot humpbacks, up close, during whale season. (If the captain makes a sudden turn, that means he's avoiding a whale, so at least look up from your book!) At other times you can delight in the flying fish and Spinner dolphins. (If you get seasick, bring along medicine, in case the seas get rough.) Reservations recommended. (Expeditions also offers "Explore Lāna'i" packages which can include golf, overnight stay, or island tours. Call for more information.)

Leaving Mānele Bay Boat Harbor aboard *Expeditions III*, the Lahaina–Lāna'i passenger ferry.

Now That You're Here...

From the airport, you can take a hotel shuttle (Four Seasons Resort Lānaʻi at Mānele Bay, The Lodge at Kōʻele, or Hotel Lānaʻi guests only) or call **Rabacca's Limousine Service** (1-808-565-6670), which utilizes a fleet of vans, stretch limos, Jeep Cherokees and a Chevy Suburban, for inexpensive airport transfers, beach transportation, hourly charters, and reasonably priced island tours. There are no other choices except hitchhiking.

If you arrive by ferry as a hotel guest, the hotel shuttle will pick you up. If you're a day visitor with no luggage, you can easily walk to Hulopoʻe Beach Park or up to the Four Seasons Resort Lānaʻi at Mānele Bay for lunch. Further than that you'll need wheels. (It's about eight miles uphill to Lānaʻi City.) Of course, if you're feeling brave, you can always ask a friendly local for a ride up to town.

Courtesy of Castle & Cooke Resorts, LLC

With only 30 miles of paved roads, Lānaʻi is a Jeep-lover's paradise.

CAR AND JEEP RENTAL

Remember, only 30 miles of Lāna'i's roads are paved, so for real exploring, you need to rent a Jeep. Since Lāna'i City itself is such an easy town to explore without a vehicle, consider renting only on the days you feel inspired to do the Indiana Jones bumpy-road-wild-adventure thing. Vehicle reservations in advance strongly recommended.

On the outskirts of town, Lāna'i City Service stands as the only gas station on the entire island.

Lāna'i City Service, a division of Dollar Rent A Car (1-800-533-7808, 1-800-Jeep808, 1-808-565-7227) rents 4-wheel drive Jeeps and minivans. Compact cars are also available. (They'll pick you up at the airport or boat harbor if you're a rental customer.) Lāna'i City Service is also the island's one and only gas station. In addition, they run Lāna'i Plantation Store, a souvenir and snack shop.

Adventure Lāna'i Ecocenter (1-808-565-7373,www.adventurelanai.com) offers 4-wheel drive Jeeps rentals which include snorkel gear, towels, ice chest, and boogie boards. Suburbans rentals are also available.

If bicycling is your preference, you can rent 24-speed mountain bicycles complete with squishy seats and insulated carrier rack packs.

For maps and brochures in advance, contact either **Lāna'i Visitors Bureau** (1-800-947-4774) or **Hawai'i Visitors & Convention Bureau (HVCB)** (1-800-GO-HAWAII, 1-808-923-1811, www.gohawaii.com).

A crescent moon peeks down on "Three-Stone" during a stunning tropical sunset.

Chapter Two:
A Deeper Look

An island steeped in mystery, Lāna'i seems perpetually shrouded, like the peak of its highest mountain, in a cloud of myth and legend. Once in a rare while, as if it were some tropical Shangri-La, the cloud disperses, illuminating an intricate past where fact often merges with fantasy.

Look back, for instance, to the fifteenth century. There you'll discover Lāna'i's most famous legend—the heroic adventures of Prince Kaululā'au. Oral history suggests that the famed young man was born on West Maui to Chief Kaka'alaneo. A highly intelligent and spirited fellow, Kaululā'au might have been too spirited for his own good. After he upset the community of Lahaina with antics like unearthing precious breadfruit trees, his father knew it was time to take action. Ten miles away, across the Pacific, loomed the deserted island of Lāna'i. Hawaiians knew the island to be inhabited by fearsome man-eating ghosts. They also knew that if anyone dared to set foot on Lāna'i's shores, he would never be seen again. So the chief banished his

---

He weke, he i'a pahulu.

It is a weke, the fish that produces nightmares.

(The head of the weke fish is said to contain something that produces nightmares. The nearer to Lāna'i the fish is caught, the worse the effects of the nightmares. Pahulu was the chief of evil beings (akua) who peopled the island of Lāna'i. When Kaulula'au, son of Kaka'alaneo, ruler of Maui, was a boy, he was banished to Lāna'i because of his mischief. By trickery, he rid the island of evil beings, and the spirit of Pahulu fled to the sea and entered a weke fish. From that time on, nightmares have been called pahulu, and a person who has had a nightmare is said to have been under the influence of Pahulu.)

son to Lānaʻi—some say as punishment, others say as a challenge to his first-born's abundant ingenuity. The legend goes on to describe how a powerful wizard gave Kaululāʻau a magical ivory spearhead. The next morning, armed with only that mystical weapon and his courage, the rebellious prince paddled to Lānaʻi and set foot on the northern shores, near Maunalei Gulch.

Weeks went by. Villagers of Lahaina feared the worst. Imagine their surprise, then, when one night they saw the bright glow of a bonfire flickering on Lānaʻi's coast. Kaululāʻau had done more than survive. He had outwitted and vanquished the cannibalistic spirits. The courageous prince instantaneously transformed from an unruly teenager to a legendary hero.

The adventures of Kaululāʻau proved to be a turning point. Archaeological evidence suggests that from that point on Hawaiians lived and thrived on Lānaʻi.

But reach back even further into the island's darkly glittering past, and you can almost hear the whispers of an ancient civilization. Indeed, several legend interpretations indicate that long, long ago, Lānaʻi was the center of a fabled super-civilization called Lemuria, sometimes known as Mu. Similar to the lost peoples of Atlantis, the huge and gentle Lemurians supposedly boasted a powerful mix of deep spiritual knowledge and peaceful energy mastery. When the Lemurian high priests sensed their culture's demise, they cast a powerful protective spell over Lānaʻi, in hopes that the island's *mana*, or divine spirit, would be forever safe. It was this act that originally created Kaululāʻau's guardian spirits, or so the theory goes.

Whether you believe any of it or not, history would show that, as Lānaʻi reluctantly entered the nineteenth and twentieth centuries, a powerful magic continued to make its influence felt.

In 1778, Captain Cook arrived in Hawaiʻi. It was in his ship's logs that Lānaʻi was first officially recorded, describing a friendly people of about 10,000 in number, living in "a dry dust-bowl."

This innocent encounter with European sailors unwittingly marked the end of Lānaʻi's

Ancient paved trail to Kaunolū, 1922.

Photo: Bishop Museum

Petroglyphs cover a boulder at Luahiwa, 1924.

Photo: Kenneth P. Emory, Bishop Museum

peaceful isolation. That summer, a terrible tragedy swept the island, spurred by Big Island chief Kalaniōupuʻu. Angered by recent battles lost on Maui, the vengeful chief launched a surprise attack on Lānaʻi, virtually wiping out the entire island. The population would never recover and life on Lānaʻi would never be the same.

At the turn of the nineteenth century, after the unification of the Hawaiian Islands, King Kamehameha the Great began spending his summers at Kaunolū, on Lānaʻi's southwestern coast. Revered as the best fishing spot in Hawaiʻi, and spectacularly situated in the shadow of thousand-foot sea cliffs, Kaunolū would

become the King's special summer residence for the next seventeen years. It was at Kaunolū that one of the King's bravest warriors, Kahekili, leapt from a towering cliff into the swirling ocean to prove his loyalty. Other warriors followed suit, and the cliff, which can be visited today, became known as Kahekili's Leap. In 1921, when Kenneth Emory of the Bishop Museum led the first archaeological exploration to Lānaʻi, he unearthed a wealth of artifacts, petroglyphs, and ruin sites, many around Kaunolū itself. To this day, some Hawaiians believe the sacred bones of King Kamehameha the Great lie buried somewhere in the area.

A community photo taken at Pālāwai Basin in 1907.

Lānaʻi or Bust!

The year 1802 saw the first entrepreneur arrive on Lānaʻi. China-born Wu Tsin came with high hopes of growing sugar cane around Naha, along the island's eastern coast. But he quickly abandoned the venture, inadvertently becoming the forerunner for similar future failures. Over the years, everything was tried from cotton to beets, dairy farms and piggeries. None succeeded. The rational explanation? Lack of consistent rainfall and fresh water. But for those more open-minded, the question remains: were those failures part of a powerful spell designed eons ago to keep Lānaʻi safe from outsiders?

Even when more "righteous" ventures were tried, they, too, met a speedy demise. Like the 1830 Hawaiian penal colony for women thieves and adulterers on Kaʻena Point. Their male counterparts were banished to Kahoʻolawe, but local lore informs us that they soon swam back to Maui and stole canoes in which to rescue the women. Soon both sexes were living together happily, back on Kahoʻolawe. A few weeks later, the generous-hearted Hawaiian people relented and sent canoes to bring all of the prisoners home, where they were reunited, and forgiven, by their families.

Then there was the Mormon attempt to colonize Pālāwai Basin on Lānaʻi in the mid-1800s. Six hundred strong sailed from Utah to save Lānaʻi souls. But, in a few years the disappointed Mormons went home. One formidable fellow, however—Walter Murray

Photo: Bishop Museum

In 1910, a small boat unloads from an interisland ship, probably at Hulopo'e Bay.

Ray Jerome Baker, Bishop Museum

Charles Gay (far left), the man who purchased Lāna'i for $100,000, with family and friends, 1912.

Ray Jerome Baker, Bishop Museum

A thriving grove of kukui nut trees, 1912.

Gibson—stayed behind. Bucking tradition (as well as the Mormon church), Gibson bought 26,000 acres to start his own sheep and goat ranch. By the late 1800s, despite the fact that Gibson's ranch touted tens of thousands of sheep, hundreds of cattle and horses, and a noisy smorgasbord of goats, hogs, and wild turkeys, the human population on Lānaʻi had dwindled to less than 400. And Gibson found himself deep in debt. Many years later, most of his goats, sheep and hogs would be killed specifically to stop the destruction of vegetation due to their overgrazing.

After Gibson died in 1898, his surviving family members founded the Maunalei Sugar Company, based in Keōmuku Town on the island's windward coast. In 1901, they began building a railway to transport the cane. With little regard for local traditions, they dynamited a *heiau*, a sacred Hawaiian temple area. Suddenly there was an outbreak of plague, and many workers fell sick and died. Then rainfall ceased and their fresh water turned brackish. The company went belly-up in just a few months.

Again and again, over the decades, eerie stories like these continually surface. In the 1970s, during the construction of a breakwater in Mānele Bay Boat Harbor, E.E. Black, the contractor, decided to skip the all-important Hawaiian blessing that traditionally launched all new ventures. When the contractor's giant crane suddenly toppled into the sea one day, local laborers refused to work. Mr. Black quickly brought in Reverend Daniel Kaopuiki, a beloved Hawaiian minister born in Keōmuku, to bless the construction. From that point on, everything went smoothly on the breakwater.

Still skeptical of that old Lemurian magic? So was a local resident, originally from New York City, who had just moved to Lānaʻi in 1993. One afternoon, while driving around town, she noticed something that made her hair stand on end. The license plate on every Lānaʻi vehicle had the same two letters preceding the numbers. Why was that such a shocker? Because stamped in metal on all those license plates were the letters MU.

Photo: Bishop Museum

Photo: Bishop Museum

Above: Loading cattle onto ship from the beach, 1921. Left: Moving cattle through fenced chute for shipping, 1921.

Photo: Bishop Museum

Photo: Bishop Museum

Paniolo, or Hawaiian cowboys, were integral in cattle and ranching operations.

Lānaʻi residents, circa 1920.

Photo: Sullivan Collection, Bishop Museum

Pineapple Dreams

Sorcery or no sorcery, entrepreneurs kept coming to Lānaʻi. At the turn of the twentieth century, Charles Gay, part of the wealthy Robinson clan that owned Niʻihau, arrived. Charles liked what he saw and immediately bought the island for slightly over $100,000. He quickly expanded the cattle ranch, importing herds from Kauaʻi and Niʻihau. Things went well for a while but, like so many others, Gay hit financial difficulties. In 1909, he sold everything but 600 acres to a consortium of businessmen who formed Lānaʻi Ranch Company. By that time, the population of Lānaʻi had shrunk to a meager 102. The determined Gay then attempted to grow pineapple. Unfortunately, he was ahead of his time, losing with that venture, as well. Meanwhile, Lānaʻi Ranch Company made improvements and things galloped along nicely, until one day in 1917, when everything went suddenly wrong. Old-timers say that some cattle toppled an ancient stone wall belonging to another *heiau*. Financial problems ensued and the ranch changed hands. This time Henry Baldwin was

Workers hand-picking pineapple, Hawaiian Pineapple Co., 1945

Kaumalapau Harbor under construction, December 27, 1925.

Barge loaded with pineapples at Kaumalapau Harbor, circa 1950.

Photo: Bishop Museum

Two cars on dirt road, 1922.

the lucky winner. Although Baldwin turned a substantial profit, he eventually sold everything, in 1922, to James Dole for $1.1 million.

With Dole's presence, things really started to cook. The savvy entrepreneur improved the cattle business. But, much more importantly, he began transforming Lānaʻi into a model plantation town, turning 18,000 acres of red dirt into the world's largest pineapple field. Supplying more than 90 percent of the planet's demand for this succulent fruit, Dole continued altering the landscape of Lānaʻi. He blasted out a harbor, erected Lānaʻi City, and built a new population with Japanese, Korean, Chinese and Filipino laborers. He created Dole Park in the center of town, complete with a bowling alley and pool hall. Then he added Hotel Lānaʻi as a retreat for the visiting families of executives. By 1930, the population had swelled to 3,000. And it is here, with the diverse colors and backgrounds of these hard-working immigrant pineapple laborers, that the foundation of present-day Lānaʻi was laid.

In the meantime, Dole continued to make successful decisions such as hiring back former ranch manager George Munro, an amateur botanist from New Zealand with a keen eye for solving problems. One morning, Munro noticed a glistening outside his bedroom window that would literally change Lānaʻi City forever. A giant Norfolk pine towered there, planted by Walter Gibson's family. The New Zealander observed how the enormous tree squeezed moisture from the passing mist, potentially a natural catchment for Lānaʻi's notoriously arid landscape. Thrilled about his realization, Munro promptly imported Cook Island pine seeds from the South Pacific and distributed them to the local *paniolo* (cowboys) working the ranch. Like brown-skinned Johnny Appleseeds, the paniolo rode off into the sunset, literally scattering seeds and planting seedlings everywhere. Today, Lānaʻi City's pine-studded streets are a cool, moist testament to George Munro's foresight.

Life on the island continued to thrive, and pineapples continued to be a juicy business. Eventually, though, like all the other ventures that seemed to have been halted by some invisible sentry standing guard at Lānaʻi's gates, the time came when even pineapples were no longer economically viable.

So what does a pineapple dream about? In the dark of the night, facing its own demise, when a trillion stars shine down on row after row of prickly plants, what does the largest pineapple field on earth secretly desire? Perhaps it dreams of sharing its sweet, tender soul, but in a grander, more spectacular form....

Aerial views of Lāna'i City from the 1930s to 1950.

Back to the Future

Enter billionaire David Murdock, the California tycoon capable of harvesting this impossible dream. In 1986, Murdock became a major stockholder and Chairman of the Board of Castle & Cooke, the owners of Lānaʻi Company. Murdock's vision was immense. He would launch the island into the twenty-first century by building an unparalleled resort destination. With more than $400 million to sow this field of dreams, construction began. Two very different hotels would be created. The Lodge at Kōʻele, 1,700 feet above sea level, would be a cool, upland paradise, and the Four Seasons Resort Lānaʻi at Mānele Bay, on the idyllic southern shore, a tropical dream come true. In 1990, The Lodge opened its doors, stunning visitors with a classical English manor design. The largest wooden structure in the state, The Lodge offers travelers everything from giant stone fireplaces to rolling horse pastures and sculpted gardens. Then came the Four Seasons Resort Lānaʻi at Mānele Bay, a Mediterranean-style palace overlooking pristine Hulopoʻe Bay, a

marine preserve, home to spinner dolphins and endangered Hawaiian turtles. Painted high on the walls of Mānele's grand lobby are two large murals depicting the adventures of legendary Prince Kaululāʻau.

Yet again, not unlike his entrepreneurial predecessors, David Murdock has encountered his share of obstacles. Enormous sums of money continue to flow into the island, producing acres of private townhouses and stunning, multimillion-dollar homes. Despite the unnerving economics, though, Murdock will not be deterred. A tough, no-nonsense businessman who accomplishes what he wants, Murdock undeniably and unequivocally loves Lānaʻi. The day his jet first set down on the island, something seemed to take hold of his heart — and it won't let go.

Certainly, life on Lānaʻi has changed. From the simplicity of an ancient Hawaiian village to a bustling plantation town, to a five-star resort destination, the island has seen its share of progress. Yet in many, many ways, the island lifestyle is very much as it was half a century ago. Things move along peacefully. Roads are still mostly unpaved. Jeeps and trucks are the vehicles of choice. Plantation houses still line the quiet streets with many-colored tin roofs. Roosters might crow in the front yard, while papayas, avocados, and orchids thrive in the back. The 3,000 residents still wave to each other as they drive by. They still stop to "talk story" in the post office, at the local markets, even in the middle of the road. In fact, a Lāna'i traffic jam can be defined as being stuck in your car behind an old Jeep as the driver chats with a friend.

Rent a 4-wheel drive and head to the deserted, windswept side of the island where kiawe forests flourish and you might as well be seeing Lāna'i in the 1930s. Hike the 12-mile trail across Lāna'ihale, the island's highest mountain, and witness the same breathtaking views of Maui, Kaho'olawe, Moloka'i, O'ahu, and the Big Island that ancient Hawaiians saw centuries ago. And, if you venture out at night to Pālāwai Basin, a few miles from town, you can still see the same trillion or so stars that once illuminated thousands of succulent pineapples.

So what does the future hold for Lāna'i? Beyond the glamorous resorts and jet-setter real estate, is this the final destiny that Lemurian priests hoped for? Are men like Walter Gibson, Charles Gay, James Dole, and David Murdock just unsuspecting pawns in some grand, metaphysical chess game?

Perhaps.

Maybe the ancient spirits have finally found a measure of peace, content at least for the moment to share their *mana*, their sweet, tender soul, with people from every corner of the globe. People who would never have tasted the island's special magic if it weren't for this long, winding journey.

Who knows? To be safe, though, it might be a good idea when you're out walking along one of Lāna'i's white-sand beaches or standing on one of the championship golf courses, and you're momentarily distracted by the heart-stopping beauty, to take a few seconds to whisper *mahalo*, thank you, under your breath.

After all, you never know who might be listening....

A magnificent view of east Moloka'i from Maunalei Gulch, one of Lāna'i's deepest watersheds.

Chapter Three:
Natural Treasures

Geology

Millions and millions of years ago, massive, fiery volcanic eruptions began shaping and defining what was to become known as the 1,600-mile-long chain of Hawaiian Islands. The island of Lāna'i itself was formed by a single huge shield volcano, which later collapsed into the sea, leaving behind just a remnant of its northeastern flank. Lāna'ihale, the island's long spine, is the top of that remnant, and it is still easy to see where the whole mountain broke away. Enormous underwater landslides, stretching over 80 miles out onto the abyssal plain, have carried away most of the rest. Rejuvenation-stage eruptions have subsequently hidden the lowland wreckage and muted the landscape. In fact, Lāna'i is still considered a dormant volcano, not an extinct one, but no future eruptions are expected, as the last one occurred more than a million years ago.

More recently, during the last ice age, Lāna'i, Maui, Moloka'i, and Kaho'olawe were exposed by lower sea levels as a single enormous island, now called Maui Nui. Today, the waters around the four islands are known to be less than 300 feet deep. In contrast, just ten miles off Lāna'i's southwest coast, the depth reaches 14,000 feet, illuminating, quite dramatically, that Lāna'i and the other three islands are like tiny summits of a colossal ocean-born mountain.

Na honu ne'e o Polihua.

The moving turtles of Polihua.

(Polihua is a place on Lāna'i where turtles come to lay their eggs.)

Lush vegetation and far-reaching views can be seen from the island's upper mountain slopes.

Vegetation

Lāna'i crouches directly in the rain shadow of Maui's Haleakalā and the West Maui Mountains. This means lots of dry forests, as well as an abundance of consistent sunshine for beach lovers.

In the coastal dry forest, which is prevalent all around the island but most dominant along the northeastern shore, kiawe (mesquite) is king. The old growth around Lōpā is something to behold; five trees could combine to completely ensnarl as many acres, growing under and over and around each other. Take a look, but wear boots; the thorns in there are ferocious.

Higher on the mountain, around The Lodge at Kō'ele and above Lāna'i City, the real enchanted forest begins. Above this point, hikers can revel in the incredible variety of eucalyptus, Cook Pine, koa, swamp mahogany, jacaranda, bamboo, sandalwood, kukui, California redwood, Monterey pine, and a score of others. It takes time to really become intimately acquainted with Lāna'i because every area has such a different mix and feel.

As you climb even higher on the slopes, the cloud forest begins and the magnificent fern comes into its own, competing heartily in the understory with wild orchids, ripe guavas, and lots of slippery Jeep trails.

In contrast, out on the northwestern plateau, conservation efforts struggle against relentless wind erosion. This area was heavily used by ancient Hawaiians and was already largely deforested when Captain Cook sailed by in 1778. Ironwood manages to cling of its own accord, at least keeping some soil down, but all efforts to restore native species are hugely dependent upon adequate windbreaks. The Kānepu'u conservation areas are some of the last remnants of a unique dry forest, given life by nearly a century of effort in very difficult conditions. As you fly over the island, it is easy to see all the windbreaks planted in the early days of the Lāna'i Company. The other areas of northwestern Lāna'i are mostly erosion desert, full of pinnacles and moonscapes; beautiful, but barren.

Another conservation effort that was made by the Lāna'i

For the tree lover, Lānaʻiʻs diverse flora continually delights.

Joe West

Cook pine

Zac Anguay

Kukui

Brian Valley

Jacaranda

Zac Anguay

Native Koa

Vegetation, indigenous and endemic, flourishes on this tiny island.

Ko'oloaula

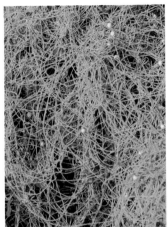

Kauna'oa

Na'u

Olopua

Exotic flowers, trees, and vines compete for attention with their dazzling array of colors and scents.

Uki grass

Loulu palm

Yellow lehua

Sandalwood

Company was the planting of Cook pines, all around Lāna'i City and on nearly every ridge top. These towering trees catch moisture from the passing clouds. Today they rise to over 100 feet and have become the island's signature tree. Surprisingly, they are only about one-third of the way through their life cycles.

Pineapple, the other signature plant, is all but gone, covering only about ten acres near the airport to serve the culinary needs of the island. The sweetest pineapple in the world, they used to say, and now it's available to only guests and residents of Lāna'i.

As on all the other Hawaiian islands, flowers also abound on Lāna'i, including yellow lehua, intoxicating ginger, fist-size hibiscus, and gorgeous bird of paradise. But the island symbol is the unique kauna'oa, a vine-like flower that appears in two varieties. One flourishes by the ocean in shades of yellow and orange, while the other, with its sunny colors more subdued, grows in the upland areas. The best place to enjoy the unusual kauna'oa flower is on your drive down to the northeastern side of the island,

heading toward Shipwreck Beach and Keōmuku.

Wildlife

Despite its small size and limited habitat, Lāna'i supports a large and diverse wildlife population. In fact, visiting hunters create a substantial revenue for the island.

Mouflon sheep, Lāna'i's bighorns, are mostly found on the dry northern and western slopes of the island, introduced in the mid 1950s. They are very alert, so look for them on ridges in the distance, preferably with binoculars, and especially on the roads leading down from Keahikawelo (Garden of the Gods).

Axis deer were originally a gift to Moloka'i from the Emperor of India and were brought to Lāna'i in the early 1920s. Twelve were released. Today there are thousands. A smallish tropical species which retains its spots throughout its life, Axis deer sport the flashy white tail when alarmed. They can be seen anywhere on the island, but especially enjoy the coastal kiawe forest. There are

Axis deer, from India, were brought to Lānaʻi in the early 1920s.

A wild baby Mouflon sheep takes its first steps.

large numbers in the upland forests, as well, and they love to slip in at night for a nibble, along the grassy fringes of Lānaʻi City. Keep an eye out while hiking, but also while driving at night on little-used roads.

Pronghorn antelope were brought to the island in the fifties, but most agree that they didn't make it. Occasionally people still claim to see them, though, so bring your high-powered field glasses, just in case.

Rio Grande turkeys can be seen all over the island. These wild turkeys were the first birds introduced to the Hawaiian Islands by non-Polynesians. Along with the turkeys, there are wild chickens that live in the upland forests as well. Peacocks roam the road, just north of Lōpā. Ring-necked pheasant and owl populations are both on the rise again. The short-eared owl, or pueo, considered by many Hawaiian people to be an ancestral spirit, flies over woods and fields, preying on mice and rats. They are active during the day but fly high enough that people often mistake them for hawks. The Pacific golden plover, or kōlea, may also be seen on the island, particularly in the area known as Kanepuʻu Preserve.

Other game birds include the Erckel and Gray Francolin which enjoy hanging around golf courses because they are attracted to irrigated spots within dry habitat. On the slopes of Lānaʻihale, along the Munro Trail, you may find Northern Cardinals, Japanese Whiteeyes, Common Myna, Japanese Bush Warbler and if you're very observant (and lucky), the native ʻApapane.

Native freshwater birds have suffered over the decades due to the loss of wetland habitat. Long ago, when taro fields were abundant, these birds thrived. Today the Hawaiian black-necked stilt, known for its rather annoying yipping call, is the only shore bird to actually breed in the islands. Look for its black and white plumage and long, coral pink legs. All the other shore birds are non-breeding visitors. A good place for spotting the Hawaiian stilt, the duck-like Hawaiian coot, and other marsh birds is the Lānaʻi City Sewage treatment plant on the southwest edge of town. These ponds attract stilts, coots, and other migratory waterfowl during the months of October through March.

If you're fishing or sailing offshore, or taking the Maui ferry, you're likely to see a variety of spectacular seabirds, including the shearwater, a grayish low flying bird whose name comes from the fact that their wingtips "shear the water" as they practically skip over the waves. Or, on land you've got a good chance at spotting the native Brown Booby roosting on buoys at the Mānele Small Boat Harbor.

So that's the good news—there are lots of interesting animals to see. The really good news, though, is that there are very few of the less-desirable, smaller critters around. There are absolutely no snakes or biting spiders. The only potentially bothersome critters are centipedes and mosquitoes; the former of which are rare, and the latter also rare, as well as a good deal less potent than their mainland kin. The one biting critter that you will see a lot, however, is the gecko, but they bite only flies, so don't be alarmed. These tiny, barking lizards are fascinating to watch; look for them at night, clinging to walls and ceilings everywhere, hanging around lights, hunting their winged prey relentlessly. Because of this, the gecko has always been well-loved by islanders as a natural pest control and as a blessing for the home. You'll see them all over the state stylized onto t-shirts, hats, stickers and surfboards.

Marine Life

Fishermen, scuba divers and snorkelers adore the waters of Lānaʻi because of its abundant and beautiful marine life. In fact, most serious diving and fishing charters from Maui bring their guests all the way to the southern coast of Lānaʻi. The superb health of Lānaʻi's fringing ecosystem, mostly due to the island's age and low human population, gives it good claim to being the nicest reef in Hawaiʻi. These

Lānaʻi's pristine coastline supports one of the most bountiful reef communities in Hawaiʻi.

Palenose parrotfish

Green turtle

Snowflake moray

Courtesy of John P. Hoover

Snorkeling in the clear waters off Maui and Lānaʻi.

Courtesy of Trilogy Excursions/ Photo: Ron Dahlquist

healthy, blooming corals cover big geologic features like canyons and sea arches. There are also lava tubes, open-top caverns, and wall dives, all in 75-to-80 degree water, with a consistently spectacular visibility range of 75 to 100 feet. Protected coastline, fantastic sailing conditions, resident dolphin pods, visiting whales, and great fishing leave Mānele Small Boat Harbor smack in the middle of the exciting action.

And it takes only a little snorkeling in front of the Four Seasons Resort Lānaʻi at Mānele Bay to get a glimpse of this undersea beauty. The bay, actually called Hulopoʻe Bay, is a lush marine preserve full of huge parrotfish, sea turtles, eagle rays, moray eels (don't touch!), and octopuses, just to name a few.

In addition, Lānaʻi is also home to a large, frisky pod of Hawaiian spinner dolphins, which often cruise through Hulopoʻe Bay and Mānele Bay as part of their daily rounds. Of all the dolphins in Hawaiʻi, spinners are the smallest and travel in

Beneath a winter rainbow, a mighty humpback whale displays its gargan-
tuan flippers off the coast of Lānaʻi.

Known for their intelligence and playfulness, a pair of Hawaiian spinner
dolphins frolic in Hulopoʻe Bay's Marine Preserve.

great numbers. This pod has at least 200 members. They are quite playful and often can be seen flipping and spinning, or riding on the Expeditions ferry bow wave. They even swim with guests, who often break the law by swimming out and inadvertently chasing them. As this often inspires the dolphins to leave the bay, it's a much better tactic to swim out to a place where the dolphins are not. There, you can relax, splash around and play, or make noises into your snorkel, and chances are that the curious pod will cruise by to investigate.

Of course, another spectacular sea mammal that is often seen around Lāna'i in winter is the mighty humpback whale, which comes to Hawai'i to breed and bear young. The high season is January through April. Whale-watchers during that time often come home awed with enthusiastic reports and rave reviews. More than anywhere else in the State, humpbacks congregate in the channel between Maui and Lāna'i. For them it's a great protected pool in the middle of the Pacific. Sometimes (especially when it's windy and rough), tour boats are treated to spectacular shows of breaching, tail slapping, baby antics, and other thrilling behaviors.

The exotic variety of marine treasures continues lavishly with everything from monk seals and leatherback turtles, to space-age manta rays with 25-foot wing spans, bus-size whale sharks (vegetarians!), bottlenose dolphins, and sperm whales.

And what about sharks, you ask? There has never been an attack on Lāna'i. For a visitor to even see a shark would be nearly unheard of. And, even then it would be a white or black-tipped reef shark which is only a threat if provoked. But caution, of course, is always in order regarding the ocean—so don't be foolish and go swimming alone at the end of the day with a bag full of bloody fish! (The most popular time for sharks to visit is at dusk, especially when the moon is rising late.) Nevertheless, remember that in Hawaiian culture, sharks are revered as *'aumākua*, sacred ancestral spirits that offer wisdom and protection.

The Munro Trail offers unparalleled hiking and sweeping island views.

Chapter Four:

Roads Less Traveled

Exploring the island of Lāna'i with a Jeep is one of the most popular activities for visitors, as only ten percent of the roads are paved and there is a lot of beauty and interest to be found in the remoter areas. Safari enthusiasts should be warned, however, that the roads described in this chapter are not always passable. This is especially true in winter, after heavy rains, and then on into spring, until the roads are fixed. They do receive maintenance somewhat regularly, however, so in summer and autumn it is usually possible to drive just about anywhere. Of course, really remote tracks can be impassable from year to year, so drivers in these areas should always be ready to let caution win the day.

(In addition, the rental companies prohibit the use of their vehicles on certain roads.)

> *I puni ia 'oe o Lāna'i a i 'ike 'ole ia Lāna'i-Ka'ula me Lāna'i-Hale, 'a'ohe no 'oe i 'ike ia Lāna'i.*
>
> If you have gone around Lāna'i, and have not seen Lāna'i Ka'ula and Lāna'i Hale, you have not seen all of Lāna'i.

Southern and Western Lāna'i

Highway 440, one of the three roads with pavement, or Mānele Road as it is usually called, heads south from Lāna'i City, and immediately drops down into the Pālāwai Basin. Pālāwai means "pond scum" and is so named because of the fog that often pools here in the mornings. This is the heart of the old pineapple lands.

Rising above the road to the left are the upper mountain slopes of Lāna'ihale, robed with ferns and crowned with towering pines.

Photo: Douglas Peebles

Photo: Douglas Peebles

Etched on giant boulders are some fascinating examples of the well-preserved Pālāwai and Luahiwa petroglyphs.

Closer to the basin floor, protruding from the lower cliff face about halfway along, are some large stones covered with the Luahiwa petroglyphs, or ancient Hawaiian drawings depicting deer, turtles, people, birds, and even a Polynesian dog. Due to unsafe conditions, public access to this site is currently closed.

On the southeast rim of the basin there are several prominent cinder cones. These are from a rejuvenation stage; they helped fill in the basin and also flowed downhill to form the peninsula between Hulopoʻe and Mānele Bays. The lava in Sweetheart Rock came from these cinder cones.

The highway soon climbs over the southern rim, a few miles west of the cinder cones, and heads down the winding road to Mānele Bay.

ROADS REALLY LESS TRAVELED:

Between the basin and the Lānaʻihale, there is a prominent bench, which forms a sort of lower-mountain highland. It is possible to explore in several locations with a 4-wheel drive. Take the first left coming down from the city as Mānele Road comes out into the basin, then fork left twice, climb a hill and go right, for 1st Bench, or Hiʻi Flats. Or, stay right on the first fork, and go left at the next, a mile later, for 2nd Bench. The upper forests of Lānaʻi are amazing and beautiful, but people rarely go. This is a great spot for hikers and explorers (and bow hunters).

Another truly astounding place on Lānaʻi that's rarely visited is Kaunolū, a huge archaeological site on the island's southwest tip. This is where King Kamehameha the Great had a summer/fishing palace (fishing off the point is fantastic—this is where the currents rejoin each

The lighthouse at Kaunolū watches over modern fishing boats as well as ancient Hawaiian ruins.

other). Hawaiian ruins are everywhere, some quite well preserved, all amid fields of sweet-smelling 'ilima, a favored lei-making flower. The famous Warrior's Leap, or Kahekili's Leap, is also here, where Kamehameha's elite warriors would prove themselves by leaping through a notch in the cliff face, and plummeting 63 feet to the water. People still come here sometimes to give it a try, but it's as scary as ever—there is a 14-foot rock ledge at water level to clear. Overall, Kaunolū is one of Lāna'i's most exciting places. It

is also the site of a *heiau*, a place of worship, and a place of refuge called Halulu, which was used by Hawaiians up through the early 1800s; Kaunolū's only drawback is the road, which fluctuates seasonally between torturous and terrifying. If you do feel brave, however, and want a little more adventure than most, turn right where the road crests to go down to Mānele and follow the dirt road which leads west along the island's rim. Keep left when the road forks after a half mile or so. At this point, start counting

A spectacular view of Shark Fin cove from Kahikili's Leap at the ancient site of Kaunolū.

Looking from Kaunolū toward the second-tallest sea cliffs in the Pacific, the Kaholo Pali.

Golden sand at Polihua beach, famous for nesting turtles, awaits the serious beachcomber.

left-turn possibilities. The road to Kaunolū is the ninth one, about three miles from Mānele Road. It should have more tracks than the others; look also for an old orange irrigation valve on the right. You'll know you made the right choice if you see an abandoned nursery a half mile or so downhill. From the turn it is about another three miles to the site. Don't forget to be extremely careful with and deeply respectful of the ruins. Try not to displace a single rock.

Highway 440 also leaves the city going west, where it passes the airport and heads down to Kaumalapau Harbor. This shipping harbor was constructed in 1926 by the Dole Company, in order to accommodate the island's increasing pineapple production. These days it sees activity only on Thursdays, though, so otherwise it's a great spot for fishing, diving, and sunsets. The sea cliffs stretching away to the north are spectacular.

Northwestern Lāna'i: Keahikawelo (Garden of the Gods) and Polihua

Head north from The Lodge, on the road to Shipwreck Beach, and turn left onto gravel just before the tennis courts. Pass the stables, and turn right at the first intersection after about a mile. For the next several hundred yards, stay on the upper track (right) if it's even a little bit muddy. The prominent ridge, paralleling the road to the north east, is part of one of the island's main rift zones, and is quite possibly part of the same collapse feature that forms the whole Lāna'ihale.

From here the road now goes six miles, more or less straight, all the way to Keahikawelo (Garden of the Gods). On the way, it passes through a strong stand of ironwood trees, and then the Kānepu'u Conservation area. Native dry forest struggles against wind erosion here, but what remains is beautiful and fascinating. A short interpretive trail, beside the road halfway

Awaiting the more serious adventurers are spots such as Nānāhoa, or "Three-Stone," which punctuates the island's dramatic western coastline.

Days off on Lāna'i are a leisurely affair; a local prepares for an afternoon of fishing at Polihua.

through the preserve, does a good job of communicating the feel of Lāna'i's ancient forests.

Just past the next gate, the area called Keahikawelo begins, better known as Garden of the Gods. This is a striking moon-scape of rock pinnacles created by hundreds of years of wind erosion. The colors here are dramatic, especially at sunset–a rich earth palette shifting from lavenders to reds to purples and browns. The legend here speaks of two great chiefs, one from Lāna'i and the other from Moloka'i. Each man built a roaring fire on opposite sides of the channel to see whose flame would last the longest. The fire of chief Kawelo won the challenge, burning strong and bright in this desolate part of the island long after the Moloka'i chief's flame went out.

If you have a Jeep, you can continue on the same road another six bouncy miles to Polihua, one of Lāna'i's prettiest beaches. Famous for nesting turtles, Polihua literally translates as *poli*, meaning bay or cove and *hua*, meaning eggs. Visit only during calm winds, however, as the sand is mostly shell particles. Occasionally, this is a good place to see a monk seal. So enjoy yourself, sunbathe, make a pukashell necklace, watch whales, but do not go swimming or surfing. The shore break and undertow are terribly powerful and dangerous, even when the waves are small. Additionally, side-shore current can be tremendous, and sharks love to hunt turtles here.

ROADS REALLY LESS TRAVELED: Follow the Kānepu'u fence line all the way around, or turn right halfway through the preserve and go down to the beach at Lapaiki. This is the spot to hunt for glass fishing floats. Or, turn right at the entrance to Garden of the Gods and head down to Awalua, where there is a second shipwreck. (There is a coastline road between Awalua and Lapaiki that might be passable.) Also, on the road to Polihua, the left turn about a half mile past Garden of the Gods, marked "Ka'ena" leads down west to a good spearfishing spot called "Red Tank." Ka'ena Point is the site of one of Lāna'i's largest heiau, which can be found by hiking about two miles north along the coast from Red Tank.

Polihua, one of several pristine
and untouched beaches waiting
to be discovered along Lāna'i's
unpopulated coastlines.

At Shipwreck beach, the concrete hull of a World War II Liberty ship dominates Lānaʻi's northern coastline.

Northeastern Lānaʻi: Kaiolohia (Shipwreck Beach) to Naha

Follow the road past The Lodge and up the hill. This road is the highway that leads to the northern coast. At the top of the hill, there is a great lookout spot on the left, especially good for sunsets.

Now the road turns northeast and climbs out onto the ancient mountain slope. It passes the Sporting Clays and an ironwood forest on the left called Mahana, an area that ancient Hawaiians avoided because they believed it was a place of evil spirits. The road then begins its long, winding descent to the sea. About halfway down it is possible to see the shipwreck, standing high on the reef to the northwest. A few miles later the pavement swoops off the arid slopes, into the kiawe forest, and abruptly disappears. Dirt roads lead away in three directions.

Behind and to the right is the Maunalei service road, which is of no interest to visitors without bolt-cutters. Maunalei is one of the island's deepest gulches; it has long been a major source of Lānaʻi's drinking water. (This happens to be a great two-hour hike, but you need to get permission from Lānaʻi Water Company.) To the left lies Shipwreck Beach, two miles away on a dirt and sand track. Lastly, straight ahead the road follows the coast for 12 miles, around to the eastern side, where it ends at Naha, another important archaeological site.

Turning left, on the way to Shipwreck, the road goes between some abandoned buildings called Federation Camp. Soon the road ends by a few picnic tables. While there's a good view of the shipwreck from here, it's also possible to walk much closer. The ship, a concrete-hulled World War II Liberty ship, became one of three Navy vessels purposely grounded here in the 1940s. The other two ships lost their battle to the unrelenting ocean. During big north swells, this one gets pounded by the surf; sprays can reach five times the height of the ship. The channel between here and Moloka'i is called Kalohi, which means turbulent and unpredictable. Indeed, many vessels have met untimely ends in the area, including a British ship and two American ones back in the early 1800s.

On the beach itself, the grooved, flat rock beds jutting out of the sand are called beach rock, and were formed and compressed beneath the ancient beach. It is a sign that the island is being slowly lifted up, even while it erodes and sinks. There is good sand here, but Shipwreck is not really much of a sitting beach.

Another highlight of the area is the petroglyphs, which can be found by following a trail west from the parking area. The trail heads slightly inland and, after about 150 yards, it reaches a small forested gully. Inside, huge boulders are covered with the old Hawaiian symbols. When you find it, there will be no doubt; it is impressive.

Leaving the pavement and going straight, the road soon curves to follow the coast eastward and, after about a mile, it comes to the roughest spot until Lōpā—up and over a bumpy hill of white rocks and back to the flat. Incidentally, although snorkeling is not so good on this whole side of the island due to wide shallows and relentless breakers on the reef, there is a spot here where it is possible, due to a deep channel. Park on the left just after the hill, and look for the spot with no breaking surf.

The road continues through mixed kiawe and coconut palm, occasionally passing an abandoned homestead, but mostly just winding in and out of the forest.

After about six miles, there is an old church on the right side of the road. Feel free to go inside. This church is part of old Keōmuku town, which can be found scattered about in the surrounding coconut grove. Keōmuku was the main community on this side of the island during the late 1800s. The church was restored once; the rest of the village is not in good shape.

A little further along is a small shrine, also on the mountainside of the road. Concealed in the forest all around here are the remains of the old Maunalei Sugar Company, which operated from 1899 to 1901, including even a small locomotive and tracks. (Rumor has it that the train was actually the downfall of the whole venture. They used rocks from a heiau to build the tracks, supposedly causing terrible things to happen. Bubonic plague hit Lānaʻi hard in 1900, and wiped out over half of the workforce. Then the water turned brackish. Within months the whole operation was abandoned. The shrine was built to honor the dead Japanese workers.)

ROADS REALLY LESS TRAVELED:
Going uphill halfway between Lōpā and Naha is ʻĀwehi Trail, a rocky and extremely difficult but spectacular way to get back to the other side. You'd better be really experienced driving a Jeep, though, as there are unexpected and sheer drops. If the road condition is bad near the bottom, it will be even worse higher on the ridge, so turn back early. One long-time local resident, a boat captain, hunter, and very skilled outdoorsman, lost his Jeep (and nearly himself and his dog) over the edge! When you get to the mountaintop, just turn left and follow the directions for the end of the Munro Trail.

Two miles further down the road is Lōpā, Lāna'i's second-best beach. Lōpā was the location of four ancient Hawaiian fishponds. The sand here is very soft, and swimming is possible, although it is quite shallow. This is a fantastic spot to learn how to surf. Hard to beat for a party, too.

Just past Lōpā, there is another rocky stretch, but then the road is smooth all the way to its end at Naha. Here, the beach is not so nice, but the fishing is great. Ancient Hawaiians lived here and built a large fishpond that is still visible, as well as many structures that can be found in the brush (be careful!). There is also an ancient walking road, paved with flagstones, that begins here and goes all the way over the mountain to the Pālāwai Basin. It is the largest Hawaiian relic in the State, and can still be followed a good deal of the way up the mountainside.

Photo: John C. Wright, Bishop Museum

Keōmuku Church stands abandoned, hidden by a coconut grove on the northeastern shore of Lāna'i.

Lāna'ihale and the Munro Trail

The Munro Trail is a rugged 12-mile track that follows the long spine of Lāna'ihale, right across the island's mountaintop. The forests are outstanding, and the views are breathtaking. On a clear day, this is the only spot in the entire State of Hawai'i where you can see five islands at once: Maui, Kaho'olawe, Moloka'i, O'ahu, and the Big Island. It is often wreathed in cloud, however, or raining, which can make the road slippery and frightening (it is quite steep in places).

Head toward Shipwreck Beach from The Lodge, and turn right at the top of the hill onto the small paved road. Pass the veterans' cemetery and the community cemetery on the right, and stay to the left when the pavement ends. Just follow the main track from there and it'll eventually take you right across the mountain.

There are many overlooks with different spectacular angles along the way, so spend some time if you have a clear day. And don't forget to sample some guava, which is the yellow fruit growing nearly everywhere around the top. Also, swamp mahogany, Monterey pine, California redwood, and Cook Island pine are in abundance, all planted by George Munro and friends to help stabilize the cloud forest.

After the summit, the forest quickly becomes drier. The soil in places is almost shockingly red. Be very careful on the downhills if it's muddy—wet Lāna'i clay is as slippery as it gets.

Near the bottom, the road switches back on itself as it comes out of the forest, and occasionally people miss the turn. Just pay attention to the gravel, and keep in mind that you are following close to the rim of the island all the way back to Mānele Road.

Left: *The rugged and verdant slopes of Lāna'ihale present visitors with exceptional views and outstanding hiking opportunities.*

Chapter Five:
Spirited Adventures

The island of Lāna'i offers absolutely no night-clubs, shopping malls, bowling alleys, or flashing neon lights. At first glance it might seem there is little to do, but Lāna'i's greatest strength has always been its outdoor adventure possibilities. Visitors can go practically anywhere on the entire island—explore to their heart's content—without ever seeing a "No Trespassing" sign. This is truly a private island, and, as a guest, it belongs to you. So claim it! You've rented it for the day or for the week—get out there and survey your kingdom.

---

*Ka ua kapua'i
kanaka o Pālāwai.*

The rain of Pālāwai [which sounds like] human footsteps.

Left: The warm, clear waters of Hulopo'e Bay's marine preserve are a constant source of fascination to snorkelers young and old.

Ocean Activities

The south coast of Lāna'i offers some of the most spectacular scuba diving and best fishing in the Pacific. Enthusiasts come from all over the world specifically to dive at the acclaimed sites called first and second Cathedrals. Visibility below the surface is almost always at least 75 feet, and the health of the reef community is unrivaled on the other islands. It should say something that nearly all of the Maui-based fishing and diving charters bring their guests all the way to southwestern Lāna'i.

On the island itself, there are several services available:

Trilogy Ocean Sports (1-888-225-6284, 808-661-4743, www.sailtrilogy.com) offers fantastic full-service snorkeling, scuba diving and sailing charters. Trilogy has been around since

Kayaking in the shallow waters off Shipwreck Beach.

The Trilogy catamarans, sailing off Lahaina, Maui.

The *Mānele Kai,* offering adventure rafting and scuba diving.

1973, so they've had a long time to perfect their game. They use three different performance catamarans ranging from 51 to 65 feet. The crew is friendly (and funny) and their cinnamon rolls are scrumptious! They offer for snorkeling, an introductory scuba class and dive, and one-tank certified dives. For more serious certified divers, trips are also offered aboard *Mānele Kai*, a powerful 35-foot, hard-bottomed inflatable. This is the boat that zips over to the best dive spots around the island (the catamarans go to better snorkeling spots and also try to get in some unforgettable sailing). One- or two-tank dives are available. If you love diving, don't pass this up. Beach diving, kayak tours, and seasonal whale watches are also available. The Snorkel/Sail excursion goes out every Monday, Wednesday, Friday, and Saturday. Other trips vary, so check with a concierge or call.

Closer to shore, **Adventure Lānaʻi Ecocenter** (1-808-565-7373, www.adventurelanai.com) offers a competitive array of kayaking, snorkeling, shore diving, and surfing in the form of guided excursions or simple rentals. While they don't have the fancy catamarans, they do have access to a lot of coastline with their expedition vehicles. Just tell them what you're interested in doing and they'll be happy to accommodate you. Rates are very competitive at around $100 per person for a half-day tour of any kind.

Also, keep in mind that the beach kiosk at the Four Seasons Resort Lānaʻi at Mānele Bay offers snorkeling and beach equipment to its guests as a complimentary service. Snorkeling right there in the Hulopoʻe Beach Park Marine Preserve can be fantastic. Two to three times per week, wild Hawaiian spinner dolphins come in to the bay to rest and play. Guests often have the opportunity to swim with them. (Please understand that chasing the dolphins or harassing them in any way is against federal law. The dolphins will come to you if they're in the mood. And they are most likely to do that if you're not following them around. Try splashing, playing, or singing into your snorkel to peak their curiosity.)

For the spirited traveler, sea kayaking is just one of the many exciting ocean activities available on Lāna'i.

Another successful day for Captain Jeff Menze (left) aboard the luxury sport-fishing yacht *Kila Kila*.

Courtesy of Kila Kila Sportfishing

Although Trilogy does a bit of light fishing about its catamarans, serious anglers definitely turn to *Fish-N-Chips* or the luxurious *Kila Kila*. They regularly catch Mahimahi (Dorado), Ono (Wahoo), 'Ahi (Yellow Fin Tuna), and of course, Marlin. Lāna'i was King Kamehameha the Great's summer fishing palace—what better place to hunt for fish! Both vessels can accommodate up to six passengers.

The 53-foot luxury yacht, *Kila Kila* is perfect for a relaxing cruise on the crystal clear waters of Lāna'i to explore the shores for secluded snorkel sites, dolphins, and humpback whales, or a magnificent Hawaiian sunset. The yacht can be rented for a sunset cruise, or for half-day or full-day fishing charter.

Reservations may be made with the **Resort Concierge at** (808-565-2387 or 808-565-4555).

Monarch butterflies enjoying the last light of another perfect tropical afternoon.

In 1993, the Challenge at Mānele's signature 12th hole was the magnificent backdrop for Bill Gates' exclusive wedding.

The Experience at Kō'ele's spectacular 17th hole drops 250 feet to the lush fairway below.

Courtesy of Castle & Cooke Resorts, LLC

Land Activities

People often travel to the island of Lāna'i just for the championship golf. It's no wonder that golf celebrities can often be seen teeing off. Both hotels offer highly acclaimed courses. In fact, The Challenge at Mānele and The Experience at Kō'ele are considered by many to be the best in the state.

The Challenge at Mānele (1-808-565-2222) more than lives up to its name. Designed by Jack Nicklaus, the course's outstanding signature 12th hole plays from a stunning cliff that rises 150 feet above crashing surf. Distances are healthy, bunkers and trees are cunningly placed and, if the ball goes onto the rocks, wish it a fond farewell. It is a stunningly beautiful course, with several holes right on the cliff edge, vines hanging down the face, soaking up salt spray from the pounding surf far below. During winter, spectacular whale watching can be enjoyed right from the fairway. The Challenge opened on December 28, 1993—the very day that Microsoft king Bill Gates was married at its spectacular signature hole.

The Experience at Kōʻele (1-808-565-4653) was designed by golf legend Greg Norman and renowned fairway architect Ted Robinson. Everything about this course is vastly different than The Challenge—from a cooler, milder climate to the misty wooded slopes, stately pine trees, manicured bunkers and terraced water hazards. The spectacular signature hole drops 250 feet to the fairway below from a tee box on the ridge. Contact a concierge to arrange tee times.

Rarely mentioned and often underestimated is a third course on the island: The 9-hole **E. J. Cavendish Municipal Golf Course,** right between The Lodge at Kōʻele and Lānaʻi City. The par-5 8th is on your right as you approach The Lodge. It's beautiful, challenging, and absolutely free of charge! A favorite spot for locals, this course of course welcomes guests to participate. To give it a try, start with the 8th hole, which tees off just across from the employee parking lot, at most a two-minute walk from The Lodge's main doors.

Non-residents are asked to make a donation to help up-keep the clubhouse. (Cavendish Golf Course is the only "free" course listed in the USGA directory.)

Ever since the old ranch days of the 1800s, Lānaʻi has been a favorite retreat for hunters. So it seems appropriate that the island now boasts a world-class sporting clays course, called **Lānaʻi Pine Sporting Clays** (1-808-559-4600). The site is fully equipped with a 100-target skeet range, a wobble trap range, and compact sporting. But the showpiece is the 14-station, solar-powered sporting clays course itself, where shooters drive golf carts from station to station and fire at clay targets in a variety of settings. Some fly like ducks, some like pheasant, quail, or doves; some of the traps even bounce along the ground like running rabbits. Lessons are also available from top-quality instructors.

Recently a state-of-the-art archery range has also been added to the sporting clays facility as well as an air-rifle gallery. Instruction is also available.

Courtesy of Castle & Cooke Resorts, LLC

Courtesy of Castle & Cooke Resorts, LLC

Courtesy of Castle & Cooke Resorts, LLC

State-of-the-art facilities at Lānaʻi Pine Sporting Clays is a unique activity for both adults and teenagers.

Guided hunts are available on Lāna'i through **Lāna'i Company Game Management** (1-808-565-3981).

Horseback riding is available through The **Stables at Kō'ele** (1-808-565-4424) which maintains a beautiful modern stable with expert staff. There are many different rides available. Contact a concierge or call.

Jeep rental is always popular on Lāna'i, as 90 percent of the island's roads are unpaved. Jeeps are available through **Dollar Rent A Car (Lāna'i City Service)**

Jeep safari on Lāna'i.

(808-565-7227) and **Adventure Lāna'i Ecocenter,** (808-565-7373) whose Jeeps are a bit beefier (and newer).

Adventure Lāna'i Ecocenter also rents **mountain bikes** and **camping gear,** and offers treks and tours of every kind. There is downhill biking, guided Jeep safaris, and hiking tours. Custom tours are no problem.

Bikes are also available from The Lodge at Kō'ele (as are picnic lunches). You simply can't beat the easy bicycling around Lāna'i City.

Camping (1-808-565-2970) is always an exciting way to experience a destination (and a great choice for frugal travelers). There is only one legal place to camp here—serene Hulopo'e Beach Park, once voted the most beautiful tropical beach in the world! Registration fees are minimal and there are nine campsites beyond the lawn that accommodate up to six people per site. The open lawn can accomodate up to 300 people. Cold showers, bathrooms, barbecue pits, and picnic tables are

Courtesy of Trilogy Excursions/ Photo: Ron Dahlquist

Courtesy of Castle & Cooke Resorts, LLC

Horseback riding, available through the Stables at Kōʻele, is a perfect way to explore upcountry Lānaʻi.

available. (Only Lānaʻi residents are allowed to camp on the sand.) These campsites are available for use on a three-day maximum basis. Call for registration and more details. Also, **Adventure Lānaʻi Ecocenter** (808-565-7373) rents a variety of camping equipment.

Lānaʻi is a paradise for **hiking**—whether you want to spend all day trekking solo across mountain tops or stroll more leisurely across sea cliffs overlooking the

Pacific. Of course, the daddy of all hikes is the 12-mile, seven-to-eight hour march along the Munro Trail that winds across the top of Lānaʻihale. If that's too demanding, there are plenty of shorter hikes available near the hotels.

Shorter hikes: Near The Lodge at Kōʻele, there are several possibilities. The prettiest forest can be found by following the service road that leads away from the clubhouse, towards the 17th hole. It crosses in front of the fairway (don't worry, the tee boxes are far above you), and proceeds into a dense stand of Cook pines. From here, a dirt road leads uphill into some beautiful mixed forests. Follow the track into the next gulch, turn left and proceed to the Munro Trail. Or climb Koloiki ridge to the right. Maps and walking sticks are available at the concierge desk.

There is also great hiking to be had in the gulch just southeast of the fifth tee box (Experience at Kōʻele course). Even if you're just playing golf, go take a look. Walk behind the comfort station, across the dirt parking area, across the road, and directly to the beginning of a path that leads down into the gulch. There is a great viewpoint just 20 feet from the road. Hikers, turn right at the bottom and follow your nose up to bamboo forests or to the Hiʻi Flats (called 1st Bench). This is a great hike, but it's farther from The Lodge than the first one.

Down at the Four Seasons Resort Lānaʻi at Mānele Bay, there aren't as many hiking opportunities, but the few that exist are delightful. First of all, no guest should miss out on walking to the point. Here, there are fascinating tide pools filled with all sorts of odd marine life, including sea cucumbers, spaghetti worms, and sea stars. The tide pools can be a glorious place for children, but make sure everyone wears sneakers or reef walkers. Also, remember never to turn your back on the waves—a piece of local wisdom that all should heed. There's also a natural lava arch that you can walk across, and a cliff side path to the overlook of Sweetheart Rock. From there, perched on top of a 120-foot cliff, you can look across and see beautiful Pehe's burial cairn (see story on next page). Also, far below is Shark's Bay, with its hidden pepper-sand beach.

The site of an ancient, tragic legend, Pu'u Pehe, or Sweetheart Rock.

The Legend of Pu'u Pehe, or Sweetheart Rock

The story behind this towering rock that rises majestically between the waters of Hulopo'e and Mānele Bays is a sad one. It seems that long ago a jealous Lāna'ian named Makakehau kept his beautiful wife, Pehe, hidden in a sea cave. One day, while he was out collecting fresh water, a fierce storm rolled in, drowning his lovely wife. Overcome with grief, he carried her body to the summit of this giant rock (some say with the help of gods), where her grave can still be seen today. Then, unable to go on without her, he leapt to his death. Some legends say that when he hit the water, he became a shark to forever guard her resting place.

A fishing boat comes into Mānele Bay Boat Harbor after a day of hunting big trophy fish off Lāna'i's southwestern coast.

Another good way to explore the cliff side in the same general area is to walk or ride to the small boat harbor. Turn right at the stop sign, then follow a dirt track which leads away from the back of a small parking area in the trees. This road leads right to the cliff, and it is easy to do more exploration. Turn left, and follow the cliffs back to the harbor; on the way you will see the remnants of the old cattle ramp used by Charles Gay for loading steer onto freighters. Or, turn right, and cross Lāna'i's best sand dunes back to the beach.

Alternately, you can hike the old Hawaiian fishermen's trail which once led from Hulopo'e all the way to the southwest tip of the island. Today it can be followed from the beach to the farthest edge of the golf course, all right along the cliffs. The trail is easy to pick out, and can even be found just beyond the lawn below the pool. It's a great hike, with history, but a hot one, so bring plenty of water. This trip is offered twice a week as a guided fitness hike, led by the spa staff.

Gene Hackman Who?

Celebrities adore Lāna'i. Whether it's Hollywood legends such as Kevin Costner, and Arnold Schwarzenegger, or sports heroes like Michael Jordan and Ken Griffey, Jr., or royalty from nations large and small, Lāna'i offers the rich and famous a genuine place of refuge and respite.

Gene Hackman once enjoyed that gentle anonymity in a completely unexpected way. During a visit to the island, Hackman and his wife went exploring by Jeep, but their vehicle became stuck in the sand near Shipwreck Beach. With no cell phones in those days, the couple began the long uphill trek, back to Lāna'i City.

Luckily, two employees of the company were driving home from the same area, when they spotted the older couple hiking up through the brush. Walter, the driver, immediately stopped, and his girlfriend, Lynn, jumped out to offer them a ride back to town. When she reached the tired, sweaty pair, the man looked up. Lynn suppressed a gasp. It was Gene Hackman! Often, she had seen him around the hotel, but, like the other employees, she never intruded on his privacy. Making an effort to appear nonchalant, Lynn invited the couple into the Jeep. Hackman and his wife gratefully accepted. Walter didn't seem to recognize the world-acclaimed Hollywood star and his wife as they climbed into the backseat. As they drove up the hill, they all began chatting and the subject of scuba diving soon came up. Both Walter and Gene Hackman were diving enthusiasts. When the actor said he had been actually certified on Lāna'i by a local instructor named Chad Bailey, Walter burst out, "No kidding?! I hang out with Chad all the time. You know, he even certified Gene Hackman!"

A thick silence filled the Jeep. Lynn leaned over and whispered, through gritted teeth, "Honey, that IS Gene Hackman."

Chapter Six:
Eat, Drink, and Talk Story

While Lānaʻi definitely does not overwhelm with zillions of places to eat, sleep, or shop, like the other islands, it offers enough of a delightful variety to utterly enjoy yourself.

Niniu Molokaʻi, poahi Lānaʻi.

Molokaʻi revolves, Lānaʻi sways.

(A description of the revolving of the hips and the swaying movements in hula.)

Accommodations

To say there are "only" three hotels on the island is to vastly understate the elegance, beauty, and charm of those three. The 236-room Four Seasons Resort Lānaʻi at Mānele Bay and the 102-room Lodge at Kōʻele are world-class, award-winning, five-star resorts offering unparalleled service, settings, and dining. The quaint 10-room Hotel Lānaʻi, the island's original clapboard plantation-style country inn, is enchanting in its own less fancy way. Guests at either of the two major hotels are welcome to use the facilities at both. Resort guests may utilitze the shuttles continuously running between the Four Seasons Resort Lānaʻi at Mānele Bay and The Lodge at Kōʻele, making an additional stop in front of Hotel Lānaʻi. (Check the times with your concierge.)

Left: *Traditional hula is performed on Kailani Terrace at Four Seasons Resort Lānaʻi at Mānele Bay.*

Sweeping panoramic views that often include humpback whales and dolphins, from poolside at the 236-room Four Seasons Resort Lāna'i at Mānele Bay.

Photo: Douglas Peebles

Courtesy of Castle & Cooke Resorts, LLC

FFOUR SEASONS RESORT LĀNAʻI AT MĀNELE BAY
1-800-321-4666, 1-808-565-7700,
www.fourseasons.com/manelebay
If your vacation fantasy is set on a stunning tropical resort with panoramic views of the Pacific and a nearby white-sand beach voted one of the most beautiful tropical beaches in the world, the Four Seasons Resort Lānaʻi at Mānele Bay is the place to stay. Ranked number two in Hawaiʻi as part of Condé Nast *Traveler's* "Gold List: World's Best Places to Stay," the hotel is a dazzling visual feast combining the sophisticated allure of Asia and the Mediterranean, and the heavenly beauty of the Hawaiian Islands.

Perched spectacularly atop red lava cliffs, this magnificent seaside villa has everything from intimate courtyards, exotic gardens, and precious Oriental antiques to massive hand-painted murals. The hotel's extraordinarily sumptuous suites offer the finest in British butler service and have housed a Saudi prince (along with his entire entourage), as well as world-acclaimed celebrities who arrive at Lānaʻi Airport in their own private jets.

Four Seasons Resort Lāna'i at Mānele Bay's dazzling lobby is a visual feast filled with rare Asian antiques and massive hand-painted murals.

The elegant Great Hall offers The Lodge at Kō'ele guests high-beamed ceilings, overstuffed couches, brocade tapestries, and the largest fireplaces in Hawai'i.

THE LODGE AT KŌ'ELE
1-800-321-4666, 1-808-565-7300, www.fourseasons.com

Yearning for a cooler, mistier, Victorian-style estate complete with rolling hills, towering pine trees, and giant stone fireplaces? Then the old-world elegance of The Lodge at Kō'ele will take your breath away. Located in upcountry Lāna'i, eight miles from the ocean, and proud to be the largest wooden building in Hawai'i, The Lodge at Kō'ele has garnered even more prestigious awards than Mānele, chief of which was the ranking of Number One in the World! (Condé Nast *Traveler's* "Gold List".) Year after year, The Lodge continues to receive top-ten rankings from sources far and wide.

A relaxed, yet refined, atmosphere, this sprawling country manor offers a plethora of delights for the sophisticated traveler. The unforgettable Great Hall is grand as well as cozy, with its high-beamed ceilings, exotic carved chandeliers, antique rugs, brocade tapestries, over-stuffed couches and armchairs, and the largest fireplaces in the state. There's also a library that provides newspapers from around the world, a trophy room to play chess (and other board games), and a

The reflecting pool at The Lodge at Kō'ele complements the serene setting of this elegant English-style manor.

Photo: Douglas Peebles

Overhead view of the 102-room The Lodge at Kōʻele set amidst cool upland forests and manicured grounds.

music room, with a hand-painted ceiling.

Outside, manicured lawns and gardens feature croquet and lawn bowling, an English-style conservatory orchid house, and groves of exotic trees. There is also a serene reflecting pool that once served as the reservoir for the farming community of Kōʻele back in the early 1900s.

HOTEL LĀNAʻI
1-800-795-7211, 808-565-7211, www.hotellanai.com

No matter how overwhelming the other hotels are, remember this one was here first, long before the island was transformed from the world's largest pineapple plantation into a world-class resort destination. Built in the 1920s by James Dole specifically for important guests of the plantation executives, this country inn has been through a few lifetimes. But after a half

Charming Hotel Lāna'i, built in the 1920s, is a cozy and picturesque country inn nestled on a hill in Lāna'i City.

million dollars in renovation back in 1994, and new ownership by an internationally acclaimed chef, Hotel Lāna'i shines even brighter while still retaining its special charm.

All rooms have ceiling fans, hardwood floors, pedestal sinks, handmade country quilts, and original pictures of the old plantation days. Don't look for phones, air conditioning, or televisions, though. (There's also the original caretaker's cottage available for rent with television, tub, and a

private entrance.) Book as far in advance as you can. Rates include continental breakfast.

DREAMS COME TRUE
547 12th Street,
1-800-566-6961, 1-808-565-6961,
www.dreamscometruelanai.com

Susan and Michael Hunter have lived around the world, but they've made Lāna'i their home for the past 17 years. Their quaint plantation bed & breakfast is hidden among avocado and banana trees. You can sleep in a four- poster hand-carved bed from Sri Lanka and wake up to fresh- brewed coffee, local fruit, cereal, and homemade bread. Both talented jewelers, they also operate a working studio on their grounds.

HALE MOE
1-808-565-9520

Momi Suzuki, long-time Lānaʻi native and gifted artist, offers three bedrooms in her Lānaʻi City home, all with private baths. A delicious continental breakfast is included. Feel free to enjoy her large outdoor deck, bicycles, and entertainment center, as well. And, if she's not busy, she's happy to pick you up at the airport. What more can you ask for?

DOLORES FABRAO
1-808-565-6134

Rents two guest rooms, one with a shared bathroom, and the other, which sleeps six, with a private bathroom. She doesn't offer breakfast but welcomes you to use her kitchen. (Ask her about the outrageously delicious homemade jams she makes, sold under the Fabrao House label at the Saturday marketplace in Dole Park. They come in a range of exotic local flavors, including pineapple-coconut, passion fruit, and papaya.)

HALE O LĀNAʻI
808-247-3637, www.hibeach.com

Offers two-bedroom vacation rentals that sleep up to six, in the heart of Lānaʻi City. Comes fully equipped with towels, linens, and kitchen utensils. Four-wheel drive Jeep available on request.

OKAMOTO REALTY LLC
1-808-565-7519,
www.okamotorealty.com

Rents single-family homes.

Lāna'i keiki and their families love to eat and talk story all day at the Blue Ginger Café.

Tanigawa's is one of Lāna'i's most cherished landmark restaurants, now owned and operated by Canoes Lāna'i.

Eating

Let's begin with the wonderful local hangouts and work our way up to the magnificent formal and informal dining rooms in the hotels.

BLUE GINGER CAFÉ
1-808-565-6363

This is the place where Lāna'ians like to talk story morning, afternoon, and evening. Cheerful outside seating looks over pine-studded Dole Park. They serve breakfast, lunch and dinner. Try their great pastries, mahimahi sandwiches, omelets, or hamburgers on homemade buns.

CANOES LĀNA'I, A Tanigawa Tradition
1-808-565-6537

This is as local and casual as it gets. This is Lāna'i's landmark café that offers a wide range of tasty choices, including its famous burgers which are coveted, even cold, all over Hawai'i! New menu items include Sesame Seed Crusted Fresh 'Ahi. Open for breakfast and lunch only, and closed on Wednesdays.

Pele's Other Garden, a New York style deli, has become a favorite among residents and visitors.

Just north of Dole Park, Coffee Works offers outdoor seating and delicious desserts.

PELE'S OTHER GARDEN
1-808-565-9628

A bright-yellow, New York-style deli on the other side of Dole Park owned by former east-coasters, Mark and Barbara, who came to Lāna'i to escape traffic jams. Overstuffed sandwiches, burritos, hearty soups, fruit smoothies and boxed picnic lunches are part of their delicious lunch. At dinner they transform into an intimate Italian bistro with real china, tablecloths, and an enticing selection of appetizers, organic salads, pastas and gourmet pizza. Indoor and outdoor seating. Reservations strongly recommended.

Note: **Harbor Café (1-808-559-0052)**, also owned and operated by Pele's Other Garden, is located at the Mānele Small Boat Harbor. This take-out snack bar opens at breakfast and has shady seats to sit and relax while waiting for the ferry or just hanging out.

CAFE 565
1-808-565-6622

This is the newest addition to Lāna'i's menu. With real pizza ovens, hoagies baked fresh every day, and genuine New Jersey talent behind the counter, this place has all the makings of greatness. Open for lunch and dinner (10 a.m. to 3 p.m. and 5 p.m. to 8 p.m.). Closed on weekends.

COFFEE WORKS
1-808-565-6962

An espresso bar and ice cream shop (on the street behind Blue Ginger Café) tempts visitors and residents with a wide selection of gourmet coffees and teas, as well as delicious bagel sandwiches, pastries, and desserts. Seating is outside on a large, quiet deck. Open for breakfast and lunch.

CENTRAL BAKERY
1-808-565-3920

This is the magic kingdom where all those fantastic breads, pastries, and unbelievable desserts are created for the hotels. It's not really a retail operation, but you can order from them with two-day advance notice.

For relaxed, upscale dining, visit Henry Clay's Rotisserie, which boasts a stone oven and the only bar in town.

HENRY CLAY'S ROTISSERIE
1-808-565-7211
www.hotellanai.com

This is a really popular, upscale yet totally comfortable place to dine, thanks to the culinary creativity of New Orleans native owner and chef Henry Clay Richardson. The restaurant, known for its Cajun-inspired dishes, is part of Hotel Lāna'i, the charming plantation-style inn that sits on a hill above Dole Park. Savory entrées range from the Rotisserie Whole Chicken spit-roasted in its own juices, to Rajun Cajun Clay's Shrimp, to hand-tossed gourmet pizzas baked in a stone oven. In addition, they've got fireplaces and the friendliest (and only) bar in town!

Four Seasons Resort Lānaʻi at Mānele Bay Restaurants

Let there be no question. The cuisine at Four Seasons Resort Lānaʻi at Mānele Bay is some of the most exquisite in the state. There are no less than four award-winning Sous Chefs on the staff to back the genius of Executive Chef Oliver Beckert. In fact, each restaurant has its own widely acclaimed chef at the helm, allowing visitors to enjoy a completely unique eating experience at each venue.

IHILANI RESTAURANT
1-800-321-4666, 1-808-565-2296

Ihilani, "Heavenly splendour" in Hawaiian, conjures images of romantic dinners for two in elegant surroundings with the Pacific Ocean as the backdrop. The refined menu, skillfuly created by world-renowned chef Jean Pierre Bellon, is contemporary Italian cuisine with a selection of fine wines that will satisfy the most discerning connoisseurs.   Choose from a wide range of truly inspired dishes such as Rare ʻAhi Tuna alla Caponata, Onaga alla Puttanesca, and Garlic-Oregano Rubbed Lamb Rack.

HULOPOʻE COURT
1-800-321-4666, 1-808-565-2290

Named after Hulopoʻe Bay, the immaculate white-sand beach gracing Lānaʻiʻs shoreline, Hulopoʻe Court is Four Seasons Resort Lānaʻi at Manele Bay's main dining room. While taking in its casual sublimity, discover myriad traditional cuisines reflecting different cultures of the Aloha State. This 145-seat ocean view restaurant is open for breakfast and dinner.

OCEAN GRILLE

1-808-565-2093

Savour delicious fresh local seafood in the al fresco ocean-front setting of the Ocean Grill. During the day, enjoy a casual lunch between laps in the adjacent pool. Come evening, start with drinks at the Pool Bar next door and continue with a seafood feast at the Grill.

THE CHALLENGE AT MĀNELE CLUBHOUSE

1-808-565-2232

Offering one of the best views on the island, the cliff-side dining at The Challenge at Manele Clubhouse is an inspiring motivator—or fitting celebration—for a day on the golf course. Savour island-influenced cuisine while enjoying ocean vistas and breathtaking fairway views. Ideal for lunch or afternoon refreshments. As you overlook Hulopoʻe Bay, you can sight humpbacks during whale season or just gaze across the water to the distant shores of Maui and Kahoʻolawe.

THE LĀNAʻI CONFERENCE CENTER

1-808-565-2424

Offers a full range of wedding, conference, and banquet options for groups of up to 500. Large numbers don't mean inferior service, though. Four Seasons Resort Lānaʻi at Mānele Bay Banquet Department is widely considered one of the finest in the State, a statement backed up by many accolades for outstanding service, set-up precision, and culinary excellence. Large-production concerts, grand firework displays, intimate astronomy parties, beach barbeques, formal dinners, complete lūʻau, and more, are all easy to arrange. The Conference Center itself offers five uniquely designed rooms (totaling 12,000-square feet), and affords panoramic views of the southern coastline. A fascinating collection of ancient Lānaʻi artifacts, gathered by the Bishop Museum, is now on permanent display, including canoe parts, coral knives, stone lamps and fishing tools, and various other implements.

The Lodge at Kōʻele Restaurants

The Lodge may not have the number of chefs that Mānele does, but it does have the extraordinary talents of Oliver Beckert as Executive Chef—and it also has the most award-winning restaurant on the island.

DINING ROOM
1-800-321-4666, 1-808-565-4580

Savour contemporary, new American cuisine featuring the freshest local seafood including Lānaʻi venison and fresh produce at the Dining Room. In a relaxed, residential-style setting complete with crackling fireplace and an impressive display of orchids, award-winning culinary delights please the palate while invigorating country air lifts the spirit.

THE TERRACE
1-808-565-4580

This has a much more casual atmosphere and is open for lunch. Depending on where you sit, you can either gaze at the antique-filled, 35-foot high Great Hall, or out at the lush, manicured gardens.

THE EXPERIENCE AT KŌʻELE CLUBHOUSE
1-808-565-4605

Sample casual dining at the Experience at Kōʻele Clubhouse, overlooking the pond at the first hole. Featured is island-influenced American light fare, which can be ordered from your golf cart and delivered to your location on the course.

Shopping

If you simply must have that "shop 'til you drop" experience, hop on the Expeditions Ferry to the historical whaling village of Lahaina, Maui, where you can spend to your heart's content. There are plenty of art galleries, T-shirt shops, boutiques, jewelry stores, restaurants, and more for a fun-filled day of emptying your bank account. Call 808-661-3756 for times and reservations.

Otherwise, enjoy these calmer offerings from Lāna'i...

Richards, the island's oldest supermarket, sells everything from hunting knives to fresh island produce.

Richard's Market (1-808-565-6047, 6789); **Pine Isle Market** (1-808-565-6488, 6775); **and International Food & Clothing** (1-808-565-6433)

All gracefully fall under the General Store category. These are the island's "supermarkets plus," where you buy everything from fresh fish, local vegetables, and canned goods, to hunting knives and fishing lures. You can also pick up all things in between, including T-shirts, greeting cards, liquor, hardware, toys, electronic games, lau hala mats, knife sharpeners, and much more. These markets can be found on the south side of Dole Park. While Richard's and Pine Isle offer a larger overall selection, International gets most of its business at lunchtime and on Sundays when the other two are closed.

On the other side of Dole Park are a few more not-to-be-missed shopping opportunities.

Gifts with Aloha (1-808-565-6589, www.giftswithaloha.com), owned and operated by Kimberly and Phoenix Dupree, who have lived on the island since 1991, is filled with unique

Hawaiian art, crafts and products. They happily ship everything from original paintings to koa canoe paddles anywhere on the mainland. Just behind, **The Local Gentry** (1-808-565-9130) owned by Jenna Gentry, is a fantastic boutique selling silk aloha shirts, sarongs, swimwear, sandals, Tommy Bahama clothing, and more. A few doors down, **The Lānaʻi Art Program** (1-808-565-7503) showcases local art and crafts, all made by talented Lānaʻi residents.

For true fine art, however, visitors will have to stop by **Mike Carroll Gallery** (1-808-565-7122), where spectacular work from various professional Maui and Lānaʻi artists is displayed. Mike himself is usually in the building working on a few new paintings, most of which are scenes of Lānaʻi that genuinely capture the old-Hawaiʻi charm of this tiny, unique island. It's definitely worth a look, located between Canoes Lānaʻi and the Post Office.

Want to really taste the community of Lānaʻi? Then head down to the Saturday morning **Lānaʻi Marketplace**, set up on the grass in Dole Park, between 7 a.m. and 10:30 a.m. Fresh produce plucked from backyard gardens, handmade crafts, garage sale items, plate lunches, fresh breads—you never know what treasures you might stumble upon. A wonderful place to "talk story" with locals.

Down the road from Dole Park, at 1036 Lānaʻi Avenue, you'll find **Lānaʻi Plantation Store, part of Lānaʻi City Service** (1-808-565-7227), which sells a variety of souvenirs, including T-shirts, pareau, necklaces, and tasty snacks, as well.

Dis ʻn Dat (1-800-565-9170), sells enchanting cools stuff for you and your place including eclectic home decor and wind-chimes.

Highlights Beauty Salon and Supply (1-800-565-7207), lighting the way to true beauty, is owned and operated by former L.A. residents Mark and Kathy Oriol. Open Tuesday–Saturday, their clients range from surfers to the stars. **Nita's In-Style (1-808-565-8082)** and **Island Images (1-808-565-7870)** are two other renowned salons on the island.

Film developing and a wide range of professional **photographic services** are available from **well-known photographer Jeffrey Asher** (1-808-565-2200). Film can be dropped off at either hotel, or at Gifts with Aloha. Or call Jeff directly.

Entertainment

If rowdy nightclubs are what you're looking for, don't bother coming to Lāna'i. This is the place for midnight walks and for extraordinary star-studded night skies (drive down to Pālāwai Basin, away from the city lights, and be rendered speechless!). But, if stargazing and moonlit beach strolls are just not enough, the island does provide a few other lovely distractions.

Hale Ahe Ahe Lounge (House of Gentle Breezes)
1-808-565-2497

Mingle and make new friends at the Hale Ahe Ahe Lounge, an open-air sports bar commanding dramatic views of the ocean. Guests can enjoy a game of pool in the Lounge's poolroom or a variety of table games in the games room, or they can simply relax and watch their favourite sports program on the 46-inch LCD television. The Lounge serves a variety of specialty cocktails and pūpū.

The Lāna'i Playhouse
1-808-565-7500

This is the place to go for movies. A charming theater built in the 1920s, this landmark building looks out on Dole Park and houses a playhouse in addition to the theater. With seating for 150, Dolby sound, and first-run movies, you'll feel right at home. They've even got fresh popcorn, sodas, and lots of standard movie fare, including Junior Mints. Before the lights go down, there is usually a lot of banter. This is a small community atmosphere, where everyone knows each other. Walking

The only movie theater on the island, Lāna'i Playhouse entertains residents and visitors with first-run movies and fresh popcorn.

through the door is often like arriving at a party full of good friends. Sometimes the entire fire department comes in to take in a flick while their shiny yellow truck is parked outside.

Lānaʻi Art Program
1-808-565-7503

This program offers guests private, semi-private, and group classes in raku, silk screening and printing, and watercolor painting.

Kids For All Seasons
"Pilialoha Keiki Camp"
1-808-565-2398

Pilialoha means close friendship and beloved companionship in Hawaiian—something we would like to share with all guests.

The program offers a full range of organized indoor and outdoor activities for children aged 5 to 12 years. There are full-day, half-day, or evening programs, different for every day of the week as well as customized theme programs.

Intended to encourage children to appreciate Lānaʻi's unique environment, the program teaches children about petroglyphs and how the Hawaiian Islands were formed. They can even build their own erupting volcano. If the outdoors is more to their liking, a game of croquet, lawn bowling, or kit flying may be arranged.

Whatever the mood, the Resort offers children the best of two worlds—water sports and highland adventures. Please contact the Concierge for schedule details.

Pilialoha Children's Program at Four Seasons Resort Lānaʻi at Mānele Bay keeps children happy and busy while their parents relax.

Courtesy of Castle & Cooke Resorts, LLC

Pampering – The Spa

In ancient Hawai'i, only the royalty, or *ali'i*, were blessed with the luxurious experience of being massaged. But, thanks to the outstanding, state-of-the-art spa facilities at both hotels, you can easily feel like a king or queen. The spa services include a full array of massage options, Hawaiian salt scrubs, specialized facials, reflexology foot treatments, herbal body wraps, aromatherapy, and yoga. Appointments should be made with a concierge of the appropriate hotel.

A stunning hand-painted mural depicting sunrise in paradise adorns the walls at Four Seasons Resort Lāna'i at Mānele Bay's luxurious spa facilities.

Four Seasons Resort Lāna'i at Mānele Bay also maintains a fully equipped beauty salon, which offers all of the standard services, as well as manicures, pedicures, body waxing, and specialized "Ali'i Scalp & Hair Treatment." Contact the **The Spa at Mānele** (808-565-2088) for more information.

About the Authors

MARCIA ZINA MAGER has been writing professionally for more than two decades. She is the author of six books, including the international best-seller, *Believing in Faeries: A Manual for Grown-ups*, CW Daniel Company, 2000. (An illustrated deck of faery divination cards will be published in German by Ansata, September 2002.)

Marcia's stories and articles have appeared in local and national publications, as well as in best-selling book series, including *Small Miracles* and *Chicken Soup for the Soul*. Featured on both American and Japanese television, Marcia has led workshops across the country and throughout Europe. In 1992, she moved from the island of Manhattan to the Hawaiian Islands. From 1993 to 1997, she lived on Lānaʻi, where she worked as editor for the *Lānaʻi Times*, Assistant Director for the Lānaʻi Art Program, and marine mammal lecturer for the Four Seasons Resort Lānaʻi at Mānele Bay. Currently, she resides on Oʻahu with her husband and son. For more information, go to her website, www.marcia-zina-mager.com.

DENNIS AUBREY has been living on Lānaʻi since 1993. When he's not writing or working at the Four Seasons Resort Lānaʻi at Mānele Bay, he's off on some long-distance wilderness adventure. Past exploits include sailing from Honolulu to Los Angeles; hiking the entire 2,638-mile Pacific Crest Trail from Mexico to Canada, solo; and bicycling 8,000 miles from the Panama Canal to Prudhoe Bay, Alaska. Currently, he's finishing his latest book, *Buccaneers in the Morning, the Truth about Angels and Elves, and a Pan-American Bicycle Odyssey*.

About the Photographer

JOE WEST grew up in Kentucky, but felt the lure of the South Pacific at an early age. He has lived in Hawaiʻi since 1989 and has made his home on the island of Lānaʻi since 1991. He has a passion for hiking, exploring, and photographing exotic, rarely seen landscapes and wildlife throughout the Hawaiian Islands. His photographs and articles have been published in magazines, travel guides and calendars. His dedication to exploring remote areas and getting "off the beaten path" has led to unique images of the Hawaiian Islands that help convey his love for the tropics. More of his images may be seen on his website, joewestphoto.com.

Right: Clear waters of ʻAuʻau channel separate the distant West Maui mountains from this secluded beach north of Lōpā.